YOUR KNOWLEDGE HAS VALUE

AF131297

Florentin Rack

Aus der Reihe: e-fellows.net stipendiaten-wissen

e-fellows.net (Hrsg.)

Band 841

Marx's Historical Materialism on Trial

An Assessment of the Historic Transformations of the Modes of Production

GRIN Verlag

Bibliografische Information der Deutschen Nationalbibliothek:

Die Deutsche Bibliothek verzeichnet diese Publikation in der Deutschen National-
bibliografie; detaillierte bibliografische Daten sind im Internet über http://dnb.d-
nb.de/ abrufbar.

Imprint:

Copyright © 2013 GRIN Verlag GmbH
Druck und Bindung: Books on Demand GmbH, Norderstedt Germany
ISBN: 978-3-656-53749-6

This book at GRIN:

http://www.grin.com/en/e-book/263955/marx-s-historical-materialism-on-trial

서울대학교
SEOUL NATIONAL UNIVERSITY

Marx's Historic Materialism on Trial –

An Assessment of the Historic Transformations of the Modes of Production

By Florentin C. Rack

"The socialist system will eventually replace the capitalist system; this is an objective law independent of man's will."

Mao Tsetung

"China's economy is now essentially capitalist, as indicated by the privatisation of the bulk of the means of production, and the conversion of labour power into a commodity. Workers can only survive by selling their labour power to an employer."

Chris Slee, socialist publicist, 2009

Introduction

In this essay I will look at states and places in which there had been (or is said to happen) a transition between different modes of production, especially feudalism, capitalism, and socialism, with the aim of verifying or falsifying Marx's historical materialism.

I will begin with a short explanation of the historical materialism and its modes of production and theoretical arguments against the concept. Then I will look at all the political entities which called themselves socialist and communist. The countries which fit Marx's definition quite well can be divided into two groups: those that were feudalistic before the transition to another mode of production, and those that already were capitalistic before the transition.

I will try to answer the question if the socialist states are becoming truly communist, or if the system is just stable, or if they are doomed to "regress" to capitalism. For the capitalist countries, I will also research their future development: if they will become socialist, if they stay capitalist, or if they will regress to some form of feudalism.

The research will show which of the possibilities have happened or are bound to happen, and therefore it is possible to say if the development predicted by Marx and Engels is realistic.

Historical materialism and its modes of production

According to Marx, the productive forces of a society (e. g. technology, land, raw materials) are owned by certain people, and the character of the productive forces that are present determine these production relations (i. e. who owns the means of production). Because the productive forces may change (e. g. the industrialization), the production relations are changed as well.

Marx analyzed the past and identified certain modes of production, which are determined by the productive forces and thus the production relations. He concluded that in each mode of production, the advancement of the productive forces led to the opposition between the ruling and ruled class growing stronger, until a revolution of the lower class started the next mode of production. In the beginning, when mankind lived in hunter-gatherer societies[1], there was no permanent surplus product and thus it was not possible for economic classes to emerge. This mode of production is called primitive communism.

The next mode of production, building on more modern forces of production such as agriculture,

---

[1] There are still some of these societies in existence, such as the Sentilese people from the Andaman Islands, who aggressively resist attempts from outsiders to contact them.

livestock farming, and trade, allowed the division of society into two classes: slave owners and slaves. The slave owners accumulated the surplus product generated by the slaves. The mode of production of the ancient society experienced some slave revolts, but was ultimately doomed because of the low birthrate among the slaves and the necessity to permanently wage war against other states in order to make new slaves. This lead to an inevitable decline in the number of slaves and therefore a crisis of the ancient society, as Max Weber suggested. Another explanation why the ancient society of Rome came to an end without a revolution of the lower classes, as Marx's theory would suggest, is that the Germanic tribes from outside of the empire were an "outside proletariat" that led to the downfall of Rome and its slaveholder society. In general, already here Marxists have some problems in defending the historical materialism empirically, also because of the fact that slaveholder societies were not present globally.

Following the ancient society comes feudalism. This mode of production is based on landowners and their serfs, which were legally dependent on their aristocratic landlords as they were entailed upon the land. The serfs had to give their surplus product to the landowners. The productive forces that led to this mode of production were more complex agriculture (e. g. three field agriculture), newer technology (e. g. wind-mills), and more intense specialization in the crafts. The term feudalism in its strictest sense applies only to European history (where the entire society from top to bottom was bound by reciprocated contracts which allowed exploitation), but similar systems existed nearly everywhere. In the French Revolution (1789), the end of feudalism in France was announced; while it came to an end in most German states in 1848, and 1917 in Russia (where it was replaced by socialism right away instead of capitalism).

The next mode of production, capitalism, is based on the capitalist class (or bourgeoisie), which owns the means of production (through state guaranteed contracts) and receives money by investing their capital, and the working class (or proletariat), which has to exchange their labour for wages and is exploited by the capitalists, according to Marx. This exploitation occurs because the wage is only a fraction of the surplus product the worker produces, and is just enough for him to survive[2]. Capitalism is associated with industrialization, modern technology, and highly advanced work specialization, and is the mode of production which is prevalent in most countries today. The capitalist system is deemed inherently unstable by Marx and Engels, because of the falling rate of profit. They furthermore predicted that the alienation of the worker with his highly specialized tasks and the exploitation by the capitalists would lead to a socialist revolution, in which the bourgeoisie is

---

[2] It can be argued that this is only true if there is more supply than demand of labour. If there is more demand than supply, companies have to compete over workers by offering higher wages or otherwise better working conditions. In this light, it is interesting to see that nowadays employers' associations in many countries demand more immigration in order to combat the declining domestic supply of labour.

brought down and the workers rule the state in a dictatorship of the proletariat.

In this socialist society, the means of production are cooperatively or publicly owned by the working class. Historically, we have seen many countries or smaller entities that called themselves socialist, although their revolutions were most of the time led by only a small group (and not the masses) or forced by foreign powers. Theoretically, socialism should lead to communism, a classless society in which the surplus product generated by everyone is used to obtain democratically chosen goals. The world has never seen true communism so far (while nearly all socialist states have moved back to capitalism). It is not possible to say if the time for this mode of production just has not come (e. g. the Greek communist politician Michalis Raptis predicted that it is at least a millennium away from implementation), or if it is just not possible and will never be implemented. The latter argument furthermore implies the question if the concept of a mode of production makes sense after all and if the modes of production and their order (as described by Marx) are a fallacy.

General criticism of the historical materialism

Some critics, such as the Marxist philosopher Walter Benjamin[3], deem historical materialism to be quasi-religious. It is not difficult to see the similarity between the concept of a Kingdom of God that will eventually come in the Abrahamic religions and the communist utopia which will eventually come in the "religion" of Marxism.

It is not possible to falsify the historical materialism theoretically, as Karl Popper noted[4]. Every inconsistency can be somehow explained away, just like the collapse of the Roman slave society is explained by the Germanics being an "outside proletariat". So all socialist countries collapsed or moved towards capitalism? It could just be the case that the discrepancy between the productive forces and the production relations is just not big enough yet for socialism to be stable, but in principle historical materialism remains unchallenged.

"Philosophy and the study of the actual world have the same relation to one another as masturbation and sexual love[5]", and therefore it is most interesting to see how historical materialism performed empirically:

[3] Benjamin, Walter (1940): Über den Begriff der Geschichte.
[4] Popper, Karl (2004): Conjectures and refutations: the growth of scientific knowledge (Reprinted. ed.). London: Routledge
[5] Marx, Karl and Engels, Friedrich (1846): The German Ideology. International Publishers, ed. Chris Arthur, p. 103

Empirical assessment

When we limit our focus on the modes of production which are most relevant in today's day and age – feudalism (including its non-Western equivalents), capitalism, and socialism (again including the different interpretations of how it should be implemented) – we can identify three groups of countries that experienced different transitions of the mode of production.

To begin with, there are the numerous countries which were once feudal and now are capitalist. These can be found all over the world, including most of the Western as well as some of the Far Eastern world. Now, according to the theory of historical materialism, they should become socialist in the future.

The second and third groups encompass those countries which turned socialist. It is difficult to assess which countries are socialist in a way Marx and Engels thought of it, as the term was used by numerous regimes[6]. The national socialists for example were definitely anti-capitalist, but then again they were anti-Bolshevist as well. And while they had a left-wing economic policy (targeted especially against banks, stock markets and trusts), they were not influenced by Marx and did oppose the idea of a class war. For most Marxist socialist movements, it is also difficult to say if they were truly socialist. Have the "nationally owned enterprises" ("volkseigener Betrieb") of the GDR really been common property of the workers? Or was it just state property, and the state was rather a new oligarchy than a dictatorship of the proletariat? Many communists deny that any country has ever been truly socialist and use the term "real socialism" to distinguish the good theory from the bad implementation. Thus they can explain away the fact that most states that called themselves socialist either collapsed economically, turned gradually more capitalistic, had a lot of inner opposition by the working class that supposedly was governing the state, or was a totalitarian rogue state (such as the Stalinist Soviet Union, the Khmer Rouge regime in Cambodia, and of course North Korea): It just

---

[6] The following states called themselves socialist:
1) Marxist-Leninist: Soviet Union, Bulgaria, GDR, Poland, Romania, Czechoslovakia, Hungary, Cuba, Albania, Yugoslavia, Mongolia, Afghanistan, Laos, Vietnam, Benin, Burkina Faso, Eritrea, Ethiopia, Ghana, Angola, Guinea-Bissau, Cape Verde, PR Congo, Madagascar, Mali, Mozambique, the Seychelles, and São Tomé und Príncipe
2) Titoist: Albania, Yugoslavia
3) Maoist: PR China, Albania, Cambodia
4) Arabian/Islamic socialism: Egypt, Libya, Algeria, Syria, Iraq, Somalia, Sudan, Yemen, Pakistan, Indonesia
5) African socialism: Upper Volta (Burkina Faso), Guinea, Zambia, Senegal, Tanzania, Uganda
6) Democratic socialism: Chile, Grenada, Jamaica
7) Moderate socialism: Afghanistan, Bangladesh, India, Sri Lanka, Guyana, Nicaragua
8) Bolivarian socialism: Bolivia, Venezuela
9) other socialisms: Burma, Albania, Hungary, PR China (Dengism), North Korea (Juche), Soviet Union (Stalinism)

was not socialism, and we should just try it again, but this time the right way!

We can divide the more feasible socialist states into two groups: those that were feudalist before they turned socialist (thus skipping capitalism) and those that were capitalist before the turned socialist. While it is not always clear to distinguish feudalism and capitalism, especially outside of Europe, and none of these modes of production was ever seen purely and solely, it seems that most of the socialist states were feudalist before. This is interesting, as according to historical materialism it might not be possible to skip capitalism. This question was also the reason for the dispute between the Bolsheviks and Mensheviks in Czarist Russia: the Mensheviks argued that a capitalist revolution was necessary first, in order to create the foundations for a later socialist revolution, while the standpoint of the Bolsheviks was that a communist proletarian revolution could happen directly. As we know, the Bolsheviks were formed into a vanguard party by Lenin and then came into power beginning with an armed riot in Petrograd in 1917 (although it was merely the Bolsheviks, not the proletarian masses, which rioted). More than 70 years later, the Soviet Union collapsed and Russia turned capitalist. Does this mean the Mensheviks were right? Capitalism as an intermediate stage is inevitable and Russia first needed to become capitalist before it can turn socialist again in some point of the future? Or is it rather true that socialism is just is not working and historical materialism, after all its little empirical inconsistencies, is finally proven wrong? Or was the Soviet Union not truly socialist and therefore it does not count and Russia just shifted to ordinary capitalism after a 70 years long intermezzo of state capitalism? Or is it theoretically possible to skip capitalism, but its time had not come yet, as only the vanguard party enforced the revolution, but not the masses from the working class?

Let us look at the possible shifts in the mode of production and what should or could happen to the countries that experienced them. There is the first group, the states that transitioned from feudalism to capitalism. According to Marx and Engels, they should have turned socialist later or should do so in the future. The second group includes the countries that were feudalist when they became socialist. They might be forced to regress to capitalism first, according to the Mensheviks' interpretation of historical materialism[7]. The third group is the one that was capitalist when they turned socialist. They

---

[7] An interesting question in this context is also how the USA should best be analyzed. Europe was feudalist when the first settlers came and founded the country as a capitalist one. On the other hand, slavery was also present, so this mode of production also existed – if you then say the USA were best described as a slaveholder society, it would mean that they might first have to turn feudalist even before capitalism can be stable. Interestingly, some people argue that a "refeudalization" is happening. This claim is mostly based on a perceived concentration of power in the hands of a few (just think of the Bilderberger conferences), the widening economic gap between the few ultra-rich people and the masses, and the dependency on certain institutions and corporations, such as the FED or the agricultural company Monsanto, on which farmers are de facto dependent for seeds, similar to the serfs of medieval Europe, who were dependent on using foreign land.
On the other hand, the regression into slavery could be seen as an unstable inconsistency, as the people that immigrated to America had already lived under feudalism for hundreds of years, and so it does not really count (after all, only about 1% of the Americans owned slaves, and the slaves in turn were also only a small minority).

should have developed communism later or do so in the future.

Examples	2	...then became capitalist, and then...			...then became socialist, and then...		
1		Progressed to socialism	Kept capitalism	Regressed to feudalism	Progressed to communism	Kept socialism	Regressed to capitalism
Was feudalist...		Sweden?	Japan	EU?	North Korea?	Laos	Russia, Mainland China
Was capitalist...					?	?	GDR

The only countries left which call themselves socialist and built on Marxism are the PR China, Vietnam, Laos, and Cuba; furthermore, Eritrea, Syria, Venezuela, Bolivia, and Belarus are led by an authoritarian socialist party, and of course there is North Korea, which is officially a socialist state, even though the Juche ideology has officially replaced Marxism. It is easy to see that all of the existing Marxist countries were not capitalist before they turned socialist, and thus I will start with these countries that once were some kind of feudalist and then became socialist. A lot of other countries belonged to this list, including the Soviet Union, Cambodia, and many African, Middle Eastern, and Latin American countries.

What did happen to the socialist states? There should be three possibilities: they could have moved on to communism[8], or moved to capitalism, or kept their socialist form. North Korea is probably the country which is often said to be the nearest one to communism, but then again, scholars rather agree on Stalinism, National Socialism[9], or even a (monarchist) theocracy[10]. Laos, Vietnam, and Cuba certainly still are socialist states and it does not seem to change to capitalism, but they had some market economy reforms and strengthening of the private sector since the end of the cold war. The People's Republic of China is an example for a country that gradually abandoned socialism, and its system could now be described as "cadre capitalism"[11]. The Soviet Union and its successor states is another example for the "regression" to capitalism – of course this time the socialist regime ended, while it lives on in China.

---

[8] Even though it's difficult to identify, as Marx and Engels did not predict how it should look like; just a classless society with the means of production belonging to the whole society.

[9] Myers, Brian R. (2009): The Constitution of Kim Jong Il. In: Wall Street Journal (http://online.wsj.com/article/SB10001424052748704471504574445980801810944.html)

[10] According to South Korean professor Yu Suk-Ryul (http://www.smh.com.au/articles/2003/03/04/1046540182732.html)

[11] Heilmann, Sebastian (1996): Auf dem Weg zu einer postkommunistischen Gesellschaftsordnung : 'Kaderkapitalismus' in der Volksrepublik China - On the road to a post-communist social order : 'cadre capitalism' in the People's Republic of China. In: Zeitschrift für Politik -Organ der Hochschule für Politik München, Issue 43/4, pp. 375-393.

An example for those countries that were capitalist before they became socialist is East Germany. Of course the socialism was forced upon the GDR by the Soviet Union, and it was abandoned after the cold war. We see the same situation for other countries of the Warsaw Pact. Cyprus was a democratic and capitalist country when the communists came into power in 2008. Nothing was changed, though, as the communist party (AKEL) is merely communist in its name: "In the Cyprian communism, Marx and Engels rather are mascots[12]". But the communist party lost the 2013 election, and so there is (not even officially) any country left that traded in capitalism for socialism and still keeps it.

When we look at the Western capitalist states, there are some warnings about them becoming socialist. If these accusations are true, it would mean that the historical materialism might be valid in this point, although Marx and Engels predicted a revolution and not a gradual transition. As an example, the Nordic states are often said to be socialist or "fake capitalist". In Sweden, for example, the government-owned means of production add up to a quarter of the Swedish productivity, and the government controls the industry through heavy regulation. But of course, the country has a mixed economy at best, and no true socialist system. Karl Albrecht Schachtschneider, Professor Emeritus in public-, and civil law at University of Erlangen, predicted in an interview in 2012 that "ultimately, a unified European state will be socialist", if the EU will one day become a real state. Especially in Europe, there are many welfare states that heavily redistribute the wealth, but the fact remains that private ownership of the means of production is legal and prevalent – and even if they are owned by state, the question remains if this means they are indirectly owned by the people or if the state is just another capitalist actor. Furthermore, it is not clear how long the welfare states remain sustainable, as an unemployed "welfare class" can live off the actual worker class. There are sometimes nationalizations or privatizations of large corporations, but this rather depends on a more right-wing or left-wing party winning the election, and does not seem to be a part of a greater trend towards either de facto socialism or "true" capitalism.

Another reoccurring reproach is that within the rich capitalist states a new form of feudalism is emerging. As said above, reasons for this prediction are manifold and include the widening economic gap between the few super-rich and the struggling masses, the concentration of international and transnational power in the hands of a few, and the huge influence possessed by a handful of large corporations, non-governmental organizations, and media. The pseudo-democratic structure of the European Union, coupled with the influence the EU has already today (for example, 80% of all economic regulations and laws in Germany come from the European commission) and the ongoing

---

[12] Martens, Michael (2012): Kommunistische Klerikalkapitalisten. In: Frankfurter Allgemeine Zeitung, 2012/07/01.
(http://www.faz.net/aktuell/politik/europaeische-union/zypern-kommunistische-klerikalkapitalisten-11805997.html)

plans to create a federal state, let accusations of feudalism appear credible to many. In this neo-feudalism, the members of the "political class", which is personally intertwined with big business, are the new aristocrats. The philosopher Jürgen Habermas identifies an endangerment of the public dialogue, because the enhanced capitalistic competition forces the media to support particular interests. The communication is limited and controlled by individual investors; the influence that states have on the public dialogue is receding in favour of the growing influence of capitalist forces. Habermas asserts that since the second half of the 20th century there is a refeudalization of the society, because not only political entities undertake certain functions in the sphere of trade and the work that is done in society, but also corporative powers undertake political functions[13]. Other social scientists see a refeudalization because of the fact that the social background is an important factor for wealth as not only prosperity and poverty are "bequeathed" within isolated social groups, but also the educational opportunities and upward mobility are determined by the social origin. Therefore, there will be a "nobility of opportunities" and a group of people without property, resources, or perspectives[14]. But, while there might be a concentration of wealth, power, and opportunities in a small group of people, the exploitation of the masses is done by the means of wage labour and not some legally justified aristocracy or land ownership. This is different to the classical feudalism of the middle ages (but then again, a too strict definition of feudalism would also exclude the non-European countries that turned socialist from analysis in the light of historical materialism). There may be at most a de facto aristocracy, which however is not legally secured and whose existence is of course denied by the alleged neo-aristocrats.

Neither the accusations that the capitalist states progress towards socialism nor that they regress to feudalism are irrefutable. It seems that capitalism remains stable. There are at least no clear indices for the transformation of the mode of production, and it may be better to see the economic and societal changes as changes within the capitalist mode of production: It just transformed into a global monopolistic capitalism which is characterized by consumerism and financialization.

---

[13] Habermas, Jürgen (1962): The Structural Transformation of the Public Sphere
[14] Forst, Rainer (2005): Die erste Frage der Gerechtigkeit

Findings and conclusion

The analysis shows that the socialist states became capitalist or are gradually transitioning towards capitalism. The capitalist states remain capitalist, although there are accusations of them becoming either socialist or feudalist, however with the accusations not matching Marx and Engels's definition of these modes of production. In the end, it just seems like capitalism (in some form or another) is the destination of today's economies. This could imply two things: either that socialism is not viable and the theory of historical materialism is not only flawed in details (like the problematic analysis of the ancient societies' end), but is erroneous in its entirety, or that we *still* have not reached the economic conditions which are needed for the forecasted socialist revolution to come and stay. The latter conclusion is of course non-falsifiable and of quasi-religious nature. Convinced Marxists could also explain away the fact that the historical materialism is not empirically proven and socialism failed by asserting that the countries which turned from feudalism to socialism had to become capitalist in between, and that the time has not come for socialism in the capitalist countries, and those countries that turned from capitalism to socialism and back (like East Germany) were only unsuccessful because they were no true dictatorship of the proletariat, but a forced expropriation and centrally planned economy, in which the means of production were admittedly not in private hands, but not in the possession of the collective workers, either, but instead belonged to the state, which acted as a capitalist entrepreneur itself.

In conclusion, although it is possible to explain away all flaws of the empirical application of historical materialism, it becomes implausible for the neutral observer. The failure of socialism regardless of the previous mode of production and the prevalence of capitalism seem to disprove Marx's theory.